Mostly Magic

by RUTH CHEW

Illustrated by the author

SCHOLASTIC BOOK SERVICES

NEW YORK · TORONTO · LONDON · AUCKLAND · SYDNEY · TOKYO

ISBN 0-590-32331-8

12 11 10 9 8 7 6 5 4 3 2 1   2   2 3 4 5 6 7/8
                          Printed in the U.S.A   11

For my granddaughter
Elsa Dunbar Sprunt

"Rats!" Emily looked out the window at the blue summer sky. "What a day to be stuck in the house waiting for a grouchy old plumber!"

Dick stood beside her. He looked out at the Brooklyn street. "I wonder how long it will be before Mr. Barstow shows up."

Emily yanked at her brother's arm. "Come on, Dick. It'll be lunchtime before we get the breakfast dishes into the dishwasher."

The two children turned away from the living room window and started toward the kitchen. They were only halfway through the dining room when the doorbell rang.

Dick raced to open the front door.

A small man was standing on the front stoop outside. "Hello. Are you the people with the leak in the ceiling?"

"You're not Mr. Barstow," Dick said.

The little man smiled. "Mr. Barstow has too much work today. He asked me to do this job for him."

Emily came to the door. She looked at the plumber. His hands were dirty and he needed a shave. But he had a nice smile. "Mother and Daddy are both at work," Emily said. "I'll show you the leak."

The plumber turned to look up and down the street. "Mr. Checkers was following me," he explained. "But I don't see him now. I hope he didn't get lost. He stepped into the front hall. "My name is Pete. What's yours?"

"Emily. This is my brother, Dick." Emily walked into the living room. Dick and the plumber followed her.

Emily pointed to a big damp place in one corner of the ceiling. "We can't find out where the leak's coming from."

"Three people have tried to fix it so far," Dick told the plumber. "Dad even had a new tile floor put in the shower upstairs."

"Leaks are funny things," Pete said. "I remember one everybody thought was from a bathtub drain. Guess what the trouble was."

"A toilet," Dick said. "Mom says I flushed my first toothbrush down ours."

"That's a good way to make a toilet overflow." Pete looked at the damp spot on the ceiling. "But the leak I'm talking about came from a radiator in the bathroom."

"There's no radiator in our bathroom," Dick said. "We use an electric heater in the winter."

"Dick, remember we have to load the dishwasher." Emily started toward the kitchen.

Dick came after her. "Don't be so bossy just because you're older than I am."

"Mother told me not to let you bother the plumber," Emily reminded him.

"I'm not bothering Pete. I'm trying to help him figure out where the leak's coming from." Dick turned to look back at the plumber. Suddenly he grabbed hold of Emily's hand and pulled her into the kitchen. "Em," he whispered, "there's something *spooky* going on!"

Emily opened the dishwasher. "What are you talking about?"

Dick's eyes were big and round. He

looked scared. "Go see what that guy's up to."

Emily tiptoed back through the dining room and peeked through the wide doorway into the living room.

The little plumber was standing on an aluminum stepladder, feeling the damp ceiling. Emily was quite sure he wasn't carrying anything when he came into the house.

Where had the ladder come from?

Emily was trying to find room for four cereal bowls on the top shelf of the dishwasher. "Pete must have left his ladder outside, and we didn't hear him go out to get it."

Emily didn't really believe this, but she had to tell Dick something so he wouldn't be scared.

"He must be awfully quick," Dick said. "We'd just left the living room when I spotted him on that ladder."

The last dish was crammed in now. Emily added the soap and turned on the dishwasher.

Crash! For a moment Emily thought all the dishes were breaking. But the sound was coming from the living room. Dick and Emily ran to see what was going on.

Pete was still on the stepladder. He was hitting the ceiling with a small hammer. The damp plaster cracked and fell. Now there was a jagged hole in the ceiling.

"Mom's not going to like that," Dick whispered. "You know how she hates mess."

Emily pointed to the floor. There was a canvas dropcloth spread over the rug to catch the falling plaster. "Pete must have brought that in with the ladder."

The plumber was looking up into the hole in the ceiling. His curly hair was white with plaster dust. "This is the quickest way to find out where a leak is coming from." Pete reached into the hole. "It's wet in there." He looked down at the children. "Did you say there's a shower upstairs?"

"Yes," Dick said, "but it can't leak. There's a new floor in it."

"Would one of you please go up and turn on the water in the shower?" Pete asked.

Both children went into the front hall. Emily turned to Dick. "Go out front and see what else Pete has left there."

She walked upstairs to the pink bathroom. There was a glass stall shower in the corner. Emily turned on both faucets and closed the shower door. After a few minutes steam began to drift out of the shower.

Emily ran to the top of the stairs and called down, "How long do you want me to leave the water running?"

Pete was on his way upstairs carrying a huge hammer. "I'll turn it off now. The leak has to be from the shower," he said. "It started raining downstairs as soon as you turned it on."

Dick came up after him. When the plumber walked into the bathroom,

Dick whispered to Emily, "Pete didn't leave anything outside."

"Then where did that big hammer come from?" Emily asked.

There was a loud bang from the bathroom. Emily and Dick rushed to the door to look in.

Pete was inside the stall shower. He had made a big hole in the pretty pink

tiles near the floor. "There's your problem, kids," he said. "It's not the floor that's leaking. It's the wall. The cement inside is all soft and wet. Whoever built this shower used the wrong kind of cement."

The broken wall looked terrible. It made Emily feel sick. Pete seemed to be knocking the house apart. Emily was sure her father wouldn't like what was going on. He took a shower every morning. Maybe he would blame Emily for letting the plumber break it.

"Can you fix it?" Dick asked. .

Pete rubbed his bristly chin. "The best way is to stuff the wall with bricks. Do you have any around the house?"

"We could look in the basement," Dick said.

Emily led the way downstairs. Pete put the big hammer on the dropcloth in the living room.

They had to go through the kitchen to get to the basement. Pete caught sight of a box of graham crackers on the kitchen table. "I haven't had any of those since I was a boy. They're great with toasted marshmallows and Hershey bars."

Dick handed him the box. "Have some. We get them all the time. I wish Mom would buy chocolate chip cookies once in a while."

Emily had opened the door to the basement stairs. She looked back to see if Dick and the plumber were coming.

Pete was munching a cracker. "Nothing wrong with these." He pulled a stubby yellow pencil from behind his ear and wrote something on the graham cracker box. Then he followed Dick and Emily down the stairs to the basement.

Emily and Dick and the plumber looked all over the basement. They found two rolls of garden fence, a stack of old newspapers, and a peanut butter jar with screws and nails in it. Pete looked hard at a chair with a broken leg. "That's perfect for a cat to sharpen its claws on," he said. "Cats like chairs better than any scratching post you can give them."

"How are you going to fix Daddy's shower?" Emily asked. "We don't have any bricks."

Pete picked up a paper bag. "What's in here?"

"Charcoal bricks," Dick told him.

"In a pinch I could use those," Pete said.

Emily took the bag away from him. "Daddy needs those to cook with when we have a barbecue."

"Never mind," Pete said. "A man is putting a new brick porch on a house around the corner."

"On Albemarle Road?" Dick asked.

"Yes," Pete said. "It's a clapboard house. A brick porch is going to look funny. Maybe I can talk him into letting me have a few bricks."

"Why don't you go and ask him for them now?" Emily said. "Then you can get started working on the shower." She opened the basement door under the front steps of the house.

"I'll take a look around for Mr. Checkers at the same time," Pete said. He went out the door. Emily closed it behind him.

She turned to Dick. "Imagine Pete thinking he could fix the wall with charcoal! He can't be a very good plumber."

"But he's such a nice guy," Dick said. "I like him much better than Mr. Barstow."

"So do I." Emily put the bag of charcoal on a shelf. "I just wish he would stop breaking up the house."

"I hope he finds Mr. Checkers. He's probably a much better plumber than Pete." Dick followed Emily back to the steps that led to the kitchen.

Halfway up the stairs there was a door to the backyard. Dick looked through the window on the door. "Something is climbing around in our peach tree."

"It must be a squirrel after the peaches," Emily told him.

"A black and white squirrel?" Dick opened the door and went out into the little garden.

Emily came out after him. She

looked up into the tree in the corner of the yard.

A large black and white cat was sitting on one of the branches.

"Maybe he belongs next door," Dick said.

"Mr. Dooley hates cats," Emily reminded him.

"Not as much as he hates kids," Dick told her. "I had to climb the fence to get my ball. And Mr. Dooley said if he ever caught me in his yard again I'd be sorry."

"Here, Cat!" Emily called.

The cat hunched himself into a fluffy black and white ball. He seemed to be trying to hide behind the little green peaches.

"Maybe he doesn't like being called *Cat*," Dick said. "If he's a stray I guess he doesn't have a name. Why don't we call him *Domino*?"

"That's a good name for a black and white cat," Emily said. "Come down, Domino. We're not going to hurt you."

The end of the cat's tail twitched, but the rest of the cat didn't move.

Emily stared up at the cat. Now she remembered seeing two sparrows building a nest in the tree. The leaves were so thick that Emily couldn't see the nest. But maybe there were baby birds in it. "I think the cat's hungry, Dick," she said.

"Mom and Dad took tunafish sandwiches for their lunch," Dick said. "The can is still in the kitchen garbage pail." He went into the house and came out with the tunafish can.

Dick stood under the peach tree and held the can high over his head. "Smell this, Domino."

The black and white cat stretched out his neck. His pink nose twitched.

But still the cat stayed in the tree.

"He must be stuck," Emily said. She always had trouble climbing down from trees.

She ran back into the house. The stepladder was in the living room, right under the hole in the ceiling.

Emily grabbed hold of the ladder and folded it up. It would be easier to carry that way, she thought.

Suddenly Emily couldn't see the ladder anywhere. A chill ran down her back. Dick was right. There *was* something spooky going on!

She felt something in her hand. Emily looked to see what it was.

Between her thumb and forefinger she was holding a tiny aluminum ladder!

Emily didn't know why she wasn't scared anymore. Instead she was excited. She had always thought magic would be fun. And now it was happening to her.

Emily looked hard at the ladder. It was exactly like the one she had just folded. There were even two tiny red steps at the top like the big ones on Pete's ladder. But this ladder was only as tall as a book of matches.

Emily unfolded the little ladder. At once it was as big as ever.

"So that's how it works!" Emily said to herself. She folded the big ladder again. Once more she was holding a tiny one in her hand.

"What took you so long?" Dick asked when Emily stepped out of the back door. "And why didn't you bring the ladder?"

"I did." Emily walked across the yard to the peach tree. She unfolded the tiny ladder.

For a moment Dick just stared at the big ladder under the tree. Then he said, "How did you do that, Em?"

"Come here," Emily said. When Dick was beside her, she folded the big ladder. Then she held up the little one for him to see. "Now, watch!" Emily opened the ladder.

Dick looked at the ladder and then at his sister. He could see that Emily wasn't scared. Dick grinned. "No wonder we didn't see Pete carry it into the house!"

Emily looked up into the peach tree. The black and white cat was still on the branch. "We'll soon have you down, Domino." Emily started up the ladder.

"I'm scared to stand way up there on the red steps," she said. "But I can't reach the cat."

Dick went up the ladder behind her. "I'll hold you so you don't fall off."

Emily put her foot on the first red step. She felt dizzy, but she stepped onto the top of the ladder. Now there was a funny ringing noise in her ears.

Emily stood on tiptoe and reached up for the cat. Dick leaned against the red steps and held tight to her ankles.

The cat climbed higher in the tree.

"Come on, Domino," Emily said. "I only want to help you get where you want to be."

The cat pricked up his ears. He looked first at Emily and then at the ladder. His green eyes gleamed.

Emily's head was going round and round. She held on to a branch of the tree to steady herself. "You know you don't want to be in this tree," she told the cat. "There are much nicer places to be." Emily was so dizzy now that it seemed as if Domino winked at her.

"It's no use, Dick. We'd better go down." Emily let go of the branch. The green peaches bounced up and down.

The cat jumped to the branch below him. "Meow!"

Emily took hold of him. Domino rubbed against her cheek and purred. She gently stroked his soft fur.

Dick started down the ladder. He

guided Emily's feet onto the steps. She was holding the cat in her arms.

Step by step the children backed down. Dick let go of Emily's feet when they were halfway to the ground.

Emily's head was clear now. And she no longer heard the ringing noise. The bright sunshine was gone. The sun must be behind a cloud. The air was much cooler.

Dick stepped off the ladder. Emily came after him. She put the cat down and folded the stepladder. At once it was so small that Emily put it into the pocket of her jeans to keep it safe.

Dick was looking around. "Em," he whispered. "We're not in our yard. Where are we?"

For a moment Emily couldn't see clearly. Then her eyes became used to the different light.

They were indoors. A big scale was hanging from the ceiling over their heads. Right in front of them Emily saw a counter loaded with all sorts of fish.

A man in a white apron was bending over more fish piled inside a store window. His back was to Dick and Emily.

"Ssh!" Emily put her fingers to her lips.

Dick pointed to a glass tank on one side of the little store. Live fish were swimming in it. The black and white cat had climbed onto the rim of the tank. He was poking his paw into the water.

Dick went quietly over to the cat. He reached out to pick him up.

Domino tried to move away from him. Splash!

The store man turned around. "I didn't see you come in," he said to the children.

Dick was trying to pull the cat out of the fish tank.

"Just a minute," the man said. "If you want one of those fish, I'll get it for you."

"He's after the cat," Emily told him.

"I don't sell catfish." The man walked to the tank.

Dick was just pulling Domino out of the water.

The store man's face turned deep red. "Pets are not allowed in the store!" He glared at the cat.

At the sight of the man's angry face, Domino made a flying leap out of Dick's arms. He landed on the hanging scale.

"Get that cat out of here!" the fish man yelled.

Domino looked down from the scale and spat at him.

Emily held out her arms. "Domino, please come down."

The cat pretended not to hear her.

The fish man reached up to grab the cat. Domino hissed and bared his teeth. All his fur was standing on end. His black and white tail was as bushy as a squirrel's.

The man backed away. "If you two don't take that cat out of my store, I'll call the police."

Emily wasn't tall enough to reach the scale. She pulled the tiny ladder out of her pocket and unfolded it. At once it was a full-sized stepladder. Emily climbed up and lifted the cat off the scale.

For a moment the store man just stared at the ladder. Then he said, "You think you're pretty funny. Well, I don't have time for your tricks. I'll show you what I think is funny!"

He tried to catch hold of Emily. She held tight to the cat and climbed all the way to the top of the ladder. The man turned around to grab Dick.

Dick slipped under his arm and jumped onto the ladder. He scrambled up after Emily. Both of them were standing on the red steps.

"I feel dizzy," Dick said.

"So do I," Emily told him. "And my ears are ringing."

Dick put his fingers in his ears. "Mine too."

"It's no use, Dick. We'd better go down." Emily called to the fish man, "Please don't be angry. We didn't mean to come into your store. All we want is to be in our own yard."

The two children started to back down the ladder.

As soon as she stepped off the red steps, Emily's head felt better. The ringing in her ears stopped.

The air was getting warmer. Emily blinked. The light was so bright now that she had to shut her eyes for a second.

Dick reached the ground first. Emily came right after him, holding the dripping cat.

"We're back in our own yard!" Dick said. "And I'm not dizzy anymore. What's going on?"

"Magic, of course." Emily put the cat on the ground. She folded the ladder and tucked it away in her pocket.

"I wonder why Pete hasn't come back," Dick said.

"Maybe he's ringing the doorbell now." Emily opened the back door. "We can't hear it when we're in the yard."

The two children rushed through the house to the front door. But there was no little plumber waiting on the stoop outside.

They went into the living room. Emily took the ladder out of her pocket. She opened it and set it under the hole in the ceiling where Pete had left it.

Dick looked at the ladder. "Pete didn't go anywhere when he was on the ladder."

"He wasn't standing on the red steps," Emily said.

Dick thought about this. "You're right, Em. That's where the magic is. You feel it as soon as you step on them."

Emily sat down on the dropcloth Pete had spread over the carpet. "I think I know why the ladder brought us home to our yard."

"Why?" Dick asked.

"Because I was standing on a red step when I told the store man we only wanted to be in our own yard," Emily said.

"You mean the ladder takes you where you say you want to be?" Dick said.

Emily nodded. "But I can't figure out why the ladder took us to the fish store."

Dick started to laugh. "When you were on top of the ladder trying to get Domino out of the tree, you told him you wanted to help him get where *he* wanted to be."

Emily thought about this. "He must have been hungry."

"And you know how cats love fish," Dick said. "I'll bet that nutty cat would rather be in a fish store than anywhere else in the world!"

Emily was thinking hard. "I was just trying to get Domino to come down from the tree. I never thought he'd understand what I said."

"He's no ordinary cat," Dick told her. "I wish we could keep him."

"So do I. But you know Daddy is allergic to cat fur. It makes him sick if there's a cat in the house." Emily got up and walked to the window. "I don't see Pete anywhere. He's not using his ladder. It's a shame to let it go to waste, now that we know how it works."

"Gee, what a great idea!" Dick said. "It's my turn to say where we go. I'm hungry. It must be nearly lunchtime. Why don't we have a picnic?"

"We'd better hurry." Emily ran into the kitchen. Dick came after her. He found a shopping bag folded up among the paper bags in the cupboard on the back stairs.

Emily packed a loaf of bread and a jar of peanut butter in the shopping bag. She put in two bananas and the box of graham crackers.

Dick added a knife from the kitchen drawer. "To spread the peanut butter."

Emily pulled two paper cups from the kitchen dispenser and took a container of milk out of the refrigerator. She tucked in a couple of paper napkins. "All set."

Dick and Emily went back to the living room and looked out at the street. Two girls had tied a rope to a fence three doors away. They were trying to jump double-dutch. The retired fireman was standing in his usual place on the corner. A lady was walking a fuzzy dog. But there was no sign of Pete the plumber.

"All clear." Dick ran to the ladder and climbed to the very top. "Come on, Em."

Emily started up the ladder. The handles of the shopping bag were looped over her arm. "Where are we going?"

"It's a surprise," Dick said.

Emily climbed up until she was standing on the red step below Dick. At once her head began to spin, and there was that ringing in her ears. Emily was so dizzy she was afraid she'd fall off the ladder.

Dick was sitting on the top of the ladder, holding on with both hands. "Ready, Em?"

"Ready!" Emily felt something soft and furry rub against her ankle.

Dick said something to the ladder, but Emily was looking at her feet and didn't hear what it was. Two green eyes were looking up at her. Domino was next to her on the red step.

Emily scooped up the black and white cat and started down the ladder.

The shopping bag brushed against her leg. A cool breeze blew through her hair. Emily heard the sound of rushing water.

She went two steps farther down.

"Meow!" The cat tried to jump out of her arms.

Dick turned to look down. "How did that cat get here?"

"We must have left the door to the yard open," Emily said. "I guess he's awfully hungry. Maybe he thought we were going back to the fish store. I wish we could find a home for him."

"Meow!" Domino tried to climb back up the ladder.

Emily held him tight and backed onto the step below. "Dick, there's water down here. My feet are getting splashed."

"Cats hate water," Dick said. "Give him to me. Then you can take off your shoes."

Emily handed the cat to her brother. "Hang on to this too." She gave him the shopping bag.

Emily pulled off her sneakers and tied the laces together. She hung the shoes around her neck and stuffed her socks into her pockets. Then she rolled up the legs of her jeans. "I can take Domino now."

Dick gave her the cat and the shopping bag. He began to take off his shoes.

Emily backed down the ladder and stepped into water up to her knees. She felt stones under her bare feet.

The ladder was standing in a rocky stream. Thick slabs of rock made a wall on one side. Deep woods grew close to the shores. In the distance Emily could see the tops of mountains rising above the trees.

The stream tumbled and splashed around the rocks. Just before it came to an iron bridge, it dropped in a foaming waterfall.

"What a beautiful place!" Emily held the cat and the shopping bag as high as she could to keep them from getting wet.

Dick was off the ladder now. He had slung his shoes over his shoulder. "Don't you remember Wangum Falls?"

Emily put the cat and the shopping bag on a flat rock in the middle of the

stream. She climbed onto the rock and
sat down. Domino crawled into her lap.

Dick folded the ladder. At once it
was not much bigger than a paper clip.
"I'll take care of this." Dick dropped
the ladder into the pocket of his shirt.
Then he scrambled onto the rock beside his sister.

"Look, Em." Dick pointed to the iron bridge. "There's the road we drove over last summer. I wanted to explore this place then, but Dad was in too much of a rush to stop."

"We were late," Emily reminded him. "Mother had lunch ready at the cottage."

Dick was staring at a dark crack between two rocks along the shore. "Em, what do you think that is?"

Emily looked hard at the rocks. "Oh, Dick! Do you suppose it's a *cave?*"

"Let's go see." Dick climbed off the rock into the water. "Maybe we can picnic in it."

"I can't carry both the cat and the shopping bag," Emily told him.

Dick reached for the cat. "I'll take Domino."

The children waded through the swirling water. When they reached the shore, Emily stood on her toes to shove the shopping bag into the crack in the rocks. She pulled herself up after it.

The crack was just wide enough for Emily to fit through. She peeked into it. "It's a cave, all right."

She lay down on her stomach in the crack and held out her arms. Dick handed the cat up to her.

Domino took a look at the crack in the rock. He perked up his ears and slipped away from Emily to run into the cave.

Emily grabbed Dick's hand to help him climb up the rock. Then she squeezed through the crack.

Dick came after her. He looked around. "Isn't this great!"

It was cool in the cave. The big rocks leaned toward each other to make a pointed roof. A soft green light flickered through the places where the rocks didn't quite meet.

The floor was rough and uneven. Right in the center there was a dent. Rain water had come through the crack in the roof and made a little pool there. The cat crouched beside it, looking down into the water.

"You won't find any fish here, Domino," Emily said.

Dick walked over to the pool. He stared into the shadows in the water. "There's something in there, Em. It looks like a lobster."

Emily got down on her hands and knees beside the pool. "That's a crayfish. It does look like a little lobster. There's another one. And what's hiding behind that stone?"

Dick leaned way over and reached

into the water to move the stone. A small black fish swam across the pool. "Hey, Em, this fish has whiskers."

Emily laughed. "A catfish for Domino!"

The cat flattened his ears and hunched his shoulders. The end of his black and white tail twitched. He got up and walked away from the pool.

Emily got to her feet. She went over to stroke the cat. "I'm sorry, Domino. I didn't mean to make fun of you."

Dick opened the shopping bag. "Time for lunch."

The children sat cross-legged on the stone floor. Emily took the bread and the knife out of the shopping bag. Dick unscrewed the top of the peanut butter jar.

Emily spread peanut butter on a slice of bread. She started to put another slice on top to make a sandwich.

"If that's for me," Dick said, "I'll take one piece of bread at a time. I like to taste the peanut butter."

"Doesn't it stick to the roof of your mouth?" Emily handed him the bread and peanut butter. She peeled a banana and began to eat it.

Domino sat beside Emily and watched every bite she took. She offered him some peanut butter. He took one sniff and turned his back to her.

"I didn't know you were coming with us, Domino," Emily said, "or I'd have brought something for you to eat."

Dick opened the box of crackers. He bit into one. "That's funny."

"What is?" Emily asked.

"This doesn't taste like a graham cracker at all," Dick said.

"We had some out of that box yesterday," Emily told him. "There wasn't anything wrong with them."

"I didn't say there was anything *wrong* with it." Dick looked at the cracker he was holding. "The light's not very bright in here. But this doesn't even look like a graham cracker."

Emily felt in the box for a cracker. She sniffed it. "Smells like coconut." She took a bite. "M-m-m, a macaroon!"

Dick was nibbling his cracker. "This one tastes like a chocolate chip cookie."

Emily picked up the graham cracker box. She carried it to a place where the sunlight streamed through a crack in the roof. "There's some writing on the box."

"Pete wrote on it with that pencil he sticks behind his ear," Dick reminded her. "What does it say?"

Emily looked at the box. There was a line drawn through *Graham Crackers*. "*Cookies*," she read. "More magic!"

Emily pulled a stubby yellow pencil out of the pocket of her jeans. "I found this on the kitchen table when I was packing our picnic."

"That looks like Pete's pencil. He must have dropped it. Let me have it for a minute, Em." Dick took the pencil and wrote FISH in big letters on a strip of banana peel.

The peel flipped out of Dick's hand and began to flop around on the floor. Now it had round eyes and a fan-shaped tail. A second later there were shiny scales on the slippery peel.

"Hey, Em!" Dick yelled. "It did turn into a fish!"

"Meow!" The cat leaped across the cave toward the fish.

"Stop it, Domino!" Emily grabbed the cat. "Dick, get that fish out of here."

Dick chased the fish around the cave. Whenever he tried to pick it up, it slipped out of his hands.

"Hold Domino." Emily gave the cat to her brother. She used the shopping bag to trap the fish. Then she went out of the cave and dumped the fish into the stream.

Emily came back with the empty shopping bag. "Now, what did you do with the pencil?"

Dick put the cat down. Domino turned his back to Emily and started to clean himself.

They looked all over the cave. Dick found the pencil wrapped up in a curl of banana peel. "I just wanted to give Domino some lunch. I didn't know the fish would be alive." Dick scratched his head. "How do you spell *sardine*, Em?"

Emily came over to help. "Let's try it with one little piece."

Dick used the butter knife they had brought from home to cut the banana peel into narrow strips.

"I'm going to make sure this one isn't alive." Emily wrote *canned sardine* in small neat letters on one of the strips.

"It sure smells like a sardine," Dick said.

Emily took the little strip of peel over to the cat. "I know you'd rather play with a live fish, Domino. But see if you can make do with this."

Domino's pink nose started to quiver. He stopped cleaning his left shoulder.

Emily put the sardine on the floor of the cave in front of him. The cat ate it slowly. When every bit was gone, he looked up at Emily. "Meow!"

She wrote on another strip of banana

peel and gave it to the cat. Domino worked his way through four sardines before he was finished. Then he licked his whiskers and walked over to Emily to give her leg a friendly bump with his furry head.

Emily and Dick were all done with their lunch now too.

"If we wrote *licorice* on the leftover strips of banana peel," Dick said, "we could save it and eat it later."

Emily thought this was a good idea. But they kept spelling *licorice* wrong and wasted all the banana peel.

"We should have written *taffy*," Emily said. "It's not as good as licorice, but at least we can spell it." She put the pencil back into her pocket. "You said you wanted to explore this place, Dick. Now's our chance."

Emily put the jar of peanut butter and the knife back into the shopping bag along with the empty milk container and the rest of the trash from their picnic. Dick picked up the cat.

They squeezed through the crack in the rock to the open air.

Emily held on to Domino and the shopping bag while Dick climbed down the rock to the stream. Then she handed him the cat and slid down to join him.

They were up to their knees in the water. It splashed around their legs.

"Meow!" Domino tried to climb onto Dick's head to get away from the spray.

Emily grabbed the cat and held him up in the air. She waded across the stream. Dick followed her.

The trees grew right down to the edge of the water here.

"Let's go for a walk," Emily said. "Put your sneakers on, Dick."

Dick sat down in the shadow of a bush. His shoes were still slung over his shoulder. Dick pulled them into his lap. The laces were tied together. "I can't get the knots out."

Emily sat beside her brother to untangle the knots in his shoelaces. Domino poked at the laces with his paw.

Crack! A twig snapped in the underbrush.

"Freeze!" Emily whispered.

A slender deer stepped out of the woods and looked around. The children sat so still that the deer didn't know they were there. She took a long drink from the stream. Then she flapped her white tail like a flag.

Two little speckled fawns came out into the open. They went to join their mother.

Dick and Emily held their breath. Domino stared at the deer without blinking.

The mother deer kept watch while the two fawns drank from the stream. Then all three bounded back into the forest.

Emily went back to working on the knots in Dick's shoelaces. When they were untangled, she handed him the shoes and started to put on her own.

"Look, Em." Dick pointed to a little path that led into the woods.

Emily got to her feet. "Maybe it's a deer trail. Let's follow it and see if we can find out where they went." She picked up the cat and started down the path. Dick came after her.

Tap, tap, tap.

Emily looked up. A little black and white bird with a red patch on his head was pecking at the bark of an old tree.

Emily could feel the cat's muscles harden under his soft fur. His eyes gleamed.

"Stop it, Domino! You're not hungry now," Emily said.

It was dark in the woods. But here and there the sunlight came through the leaves and made bright patches on the soft ground.

A chipmunk squeaked and ran across the path. Domino tried to jump out of Emily's arms. She held him tight.

"What's that on the tree over there?" Dick asked.

"It looks like a sign." Emily left the path and pushed through a clump of blueberry bushes to get to the tree.

Dick was right behind her.

"NO HUNTING," Dick read. "Do you hear that, Domino?"

Emily was reading the small print. "It says *No trespassing* too. And if they catch anybody in these woods, they fine them or put them in jail. We'd better get out of here, Dick."

"Anyway, it's time we went home." Dick reached into his shirt pocket.

"Hurry up," Emily said. "Open the ladder."

Dick went on feeling around in his pocket. Emily looked at him. "What's the matter?"

Dick looked sick. "The ladder must have fallen out of my pocket. It's gone, Em."

A bluejay screamed overhead. Emily held tight to the cat. But she got down on her hands and knees beside Dick to help him look for the ladder.

There was no sign of it among the pine needles on the ground.

"The ladder's so small," Emily said, "we'll never find it. We'd better get out of these woods before anybody sees us here."

"Listen!" Dick said.

Emily heard the motor of a car.

"The road can't be far away." Dick started in the direction of the sound.

Emily went after him, carrying the cat. They crossed a ridge and found themselves on a narrow road. Huge trees grew on each side of it. The

branches curved over the road to make
a leafy tunnel. There were no cars in
sight now.

"Nobody can fine us or put us in jail
if we stay on the road," Dick said.

Emily was scared. She knew they
were a long way from home. But there
was no sense in letting Dick know she

was afraid. They walked along the road under the arching branches. Domino seemed to get heavier all the time.

A wind was blowing through the trees now. The sunlight no longer flickered down between the leaves. Far off they heard a rumble of thunder. Emily knew it wasn't safe to be in the woods during a storm.

All at once the road came out of the woods onto an iron bridge. Under the bridge the water tumbled and splashed.

"We're right back at Wangum Falls." Dick walked onto the bridge. "There's our cave, Em." He pointed to the wall of rocks on one side of the stream. "We can see it from here."

"But we couldn't see *those* from the cave," Emily told him.

Dick looked to see what she was talking about.

There were big signs on each side of

the bridge, like the sign they had found on the tree.

"You're not allowed to wade in the stream," Emily said. "It's a good thing nobody saw us."

The sky was very dark now. A streak of lightning zig-zagged across the clouds. A second later the children heard a loud clap of thunder.

Emily felt a drop of rain on her nose. Another splashed on her cheek. Domino jumped out of her arms and raced across the bridge.

Emily and Dick ran after him.

The cat left the road and leaped to the rocks along the stream.

Emily looked at the big signs. She knew she'd be in trouble if anyone saw her down by the stream. But she couldn't let Domino get lost in the woods. Then he'd *have* to eat the birds and chipmunks.

"There's a car coming," Dick said. "Somebody will see us."

Emily was already making her way down the steep bank. Dick followed her.

Domino was leaping from one rock to another along the stream. The two children chased after him.

There was another flash of lightning and a bang of thunder. The rain was coming down in white sheets.

Domino had jumped onto a rock in the stream. The water swirled all around him.

Emily waded into the water, shoes and all. She grabbed the cat.

"Hey, Em," Dick yelled. "Look where we are."

Emily turned to look at her brother. He was standing right by the crack in the rock that led to the cave. "Come on up here, Em."

She held the cat in her arms and waded to the rock. Dick lay on his stomach and reached down for Domino. Emily handed up the cat and climbed after him.

Dick carried Domino through the crack. And Emily squeezed into the cave behind them.

It felt like coming home.

Rain dripped through the open places in the roof. Now and then a flash of lightning lit the dim cave for a second. Dick and Emily sat close to the walls, out of the way of the drips. Dick put the shopping bag on the ground near them.

The legs of Emily's jeans were soaking wet. So were her shoes and socks. Domino was wet too, but he ran over to the pool in the center of the cave.

"Take a look at that crazy cat," Dick said. "He's fishing again!"

For a while Domino just stared into the pool. Then he poked in a black and white paw. He pulled it out almost at once and started to shake it. "Meow!"

"There's something stuck on his paw." Dick ran over to see what it was. "A crayfish."

Emily went to help. The crayfish was pinching Domino's furry paw with one of its sharp claws.

"Watch out it doesn't grab you, Em!" Dick went to the shopping bag. He took out the butter knife and brought it over to pry the crayfish's claw open. "I'll have you free in a moment, Domino."

Dick wiggled the knife in the claw. The crayfish opened its claw, and Domino pulled his paw out. Dick put down the knife, picked up the cat, and began to stroke him.

Emily looked at the crayfish. "There's something in its other claw."

The crayfish was crawling back toward the pool of water.

Suddenly Domino twisted out of Dick's arms and jumped toward the pool. He reached the water before the crayfish did and crouched on the edge. "Meow!"

"He's trying to tell us something," Emily said.

The cat was moving back and forth in front of the pool. He seemed to be try-

ing to keep the crayfish from getting into the water.

Emily picked up the butter knife. She pried open the other claw of the crayfish. Something small and shiny dropped onto the floor of the cave. Dick picked it up.

Domino stood up and stretched.

Splash! The crayfish dived into the water and disappeared under a stone.

"We don't want to lose this." Emily put the knife back into the shopping bag. "We're in enough trouble already."

Dick was looking at the little object the crayfish had dropped.

"What is it?" Emily asked.

"It's so dark in here I can't be sure," he said. "And anyway it seems too good to be true."

Emily felt her heart pound inside her. She was so excited she could hardly speak. "Give it to me."

Dick handed her the little shiny thing. She held it up.

A flash of lightning lit the cave. Now the children could see that what they hoped was really true.

Emily was holding the little step-ladder in her hand.

"The ladder must have fallen into the pool when I was looking at the catfish," Dick said. "Anyway, now that we've got it back, let's go home."

Emily looked at the low roof of the cave. "The ladder's too tall for us to open it here. And we might be struck by lightning if we took it outside."

"The cave's wide enough to open the ladder sideways on the floor," Dick told her.

"But then we couldn't go *up* to the red steps," Emily pointed out.

Dick thought for a minute. "Maybe just touching the red steps works the magic."

"It's worth a try," Emily said. She laid the little ladder on its side near the pool and opened it while it was still on the ground.

At once a full-sized ladder stretched from one wall of the cave to the other. It went right over the pool of water in the center.

Dick picked up the cat. He walked over to the end of the ladder and got up to stand on the side of the red step there. Emily went to get the shopping bag. She stood on the side of the step next to her brother.

"We want to go home," Dick said. Then he hopped off the ladder.

"We're still in the cave, Em. I guess the magic doesn't work when the ladder's on its side." He put the cat on the ground.

Emily stepped down. "Help me fold it up, Dick."

"Meow!" Domino ran to the other end of the ladder. He jumped onto the edge and tiptoed along it, crossing the pool as if he were on a bridge. When he reached the red steps, the cat sat down on the side of the ladder.

Emily looked at him. Domino was swaying, and his green eyes were crossed. "He's dizzy, Dick! Hurry up! He's showing us how to work the magic!"

Emily went to the opposite end of the ladder and crawled along. The ladder creaked and shook. Emily nearly fell into the pool of water when she had to cross it. The handles of the shopping bag were looped over her arm, and the bag flapped against the ladder.

At last Emily got to the first red step. She felt it with her fingers, and bells started to ring in her ears. She crawled over to the cat.

Emily took hold of the red step at the end of the ladder. Now the cave

was turning like a merry-go-round.

Dick started along the ladder. He had even more trouble than Emily. The ladder was shaking as if it would fall apart at any moment.

It seemed an age before Dick reached the red step next to Emily. "Try it now, Em."

Emily closed her eyes and whispered, "Home, please take us home!"

She opened her eyes. "Dick," she said, "I think we have to back all the way across the ladder."

"Yipe!" Dick started crawling backward the way he had come.

Emily waited until her brother was almost to the end of the ladder before she started to move. Then she backed slowly over the pool of water.

Domino was still crouching on the side of the red step. Without any warning, he made a mad dash and bumped into Emily. The ladder tipped over and threw Emily and the cat on top of Dick.

They rolled over and over on the living room rug.

Emily let go of the shopping bag. She stood up and looked around the room. The canvas dropcloth was still spread on the rug under the hole Pete had made in the ceiling. "We'd better put the ladder back where it was. Give me a hand with it, Dick."

Dick got to his feet. He helped Emily set the ladder upright.

"Pete's probably waiting on the front stoop." Dick ran to the door. "He's not there."

"Maybe he came back and went away again. We've been gone a long time." Emily moved the ladder onto the dropcloth. She stumbled over something. It was the big hammer Pete had used to break the wall of the shower.

"Let me take that out of your way." Dick tugged at the hammer. "It's heavier than I thought." He looked at the wooden handle. "There are some numbers written here."

Emily set the ladder under the hole in the ceiling. She came over to see what Dick was talking about.

28" was marked in pencil on the handle.

"That means twenty-eight inches," Emily said.

Dick looked at the hammer. "I remember now. We learned that in school. This hammer looks about twenty-eight inches long. Hey, Em, you know what I think?"

Emily pulled the yellow pencil stub out of her pocket. There was an eraser on the end of it.

As soon as she touched the pencil

marks with the eraser, they vanished. Then Emily wrote 10″ on the handle. At once the hammer was only ten inches long.

Dick picked up the little hammer. "Now we know where Pete got the big hammer," he said.

"Yes. And I'd better make it big again before he gets back." Emily erased the numbers she had written.

"Wait a minute!" Dick put the little hammer on the floor. "I don't want to be holding this when you change it back."

Emily bent over and wrote 28″ on the wooden handle. Once again the hammer was too big for them to lift.

"Where's Domino?" Dick asked.

Emily picked up the shopping bag. "That reminds me. Go shut the back door." She walked into the kitchen and took the peanut butter jar and the graham cracker box out of the shopping bag.

She used the eraser on Pete's pencil to remove the writing on the box. Her mother would ask a lot of questions if she found cookies in it. Emily opened the box and sniffed. The smell of graham crackers met her nose. She put the pencil stub away in her pocket.

Dick had gone down the stairs to the door to the yard. Now he came back into the kitchen. "I shut the door, but I didn't see Domino in the yard."

"Maybe he's still in the house," Emily said. "We have to make sure he's out."

"It wouldn't make Dad sick if we kept the cat in the yard," Dick said. "We could build a kennel for him."

Emily didn't think Domino would want to live in a kennel, but she didn't feel like arguing with Dick.

"I'll look in the basement," Dick said. "You check around here."

Emily searched the kitchen and dining room. She looked under the living room sofa and in the hall closet. She didn't find the cat.

Dick came up from the basement. "Do you think he could have gone up to the bedrooms?"

Emily ran up the stairs. Dick was right behind her.

The children looked in their bedrooms. Then they both tiptoed into their parents' big room at the front of the house.

The sun streamed through the tall bay windows onto the wide bed. The wet black and white cat was curled up in a patch of sunlight on their mother's pillow.

"Domino!" Emily yelled. "Get off there!"

The cat opened his eyes. Dick walked over to pick him up. But Domino made a flying leap to the floor and ran out of the room.

Emily and Dick chased after him.

Emily and Dick rushed out of their parents' room into the hall. Domino was already out of sight. They looked into the pink bathroom. The cat was slipping through the open door of the stall shower.

The children ran into the bathroom. They were just in time to see the end of Domino's black and white tail disappear into the jagged hole in the wall.

Dick got down on his hands and knees on the shower floor. He looked into the hole. "It's like a little tunnel." Dick stood up. "What did you do with Pete's pencil, Em?"

Emily took it out of her pocket. "Why?"

"I want to try something." Dick took the pencil out of her hand. Emily saw him write 3½" on the back of his arm.

The pencil clattered to the floor. Emily couldn't see Dick anywhere. But when she bent over to pick up the pencil, there was a tiny boy standing in the middle of the shower stall.

"Hey, Em, it worked!" the boy said. It was Dick's voice, but not nearly as loud as usual. "Now I can find out where the tunnel goes." He ran over to the hole in the wall and stepped into it.

"Dick, come back!" Emily called after him.

There was no answer.

Emily crouched down to look into the hole. It was very dark inside. "Dick, can you hear me?"

Dick didn't answer. Emily wished she hadn't let him have the pencil. It would be terrible if anything happened to her little brother. She had to get him to come back.

Emily went to her room to get the little red flashlight she kept under her pillow. She pushed it way down into the pocket of her jeans. Then she ran back to the bathroom and stepped into the shower stall.

She stared at the magic pencil and thought hard. Emily liked being taller than her brother. She wrote 4″ on her arm.

At once the pencil stub was almost as big as she was. Emily had to drop it. She pulled her flashlight out of her pocket and turned it on. Emily took a deep breath and stepped into the tunnel.

Her shoes and socks and the legs of her jeans were still damp. "Maybe I should have written *dry* on them with Pete's pencil," she thought. But it was too late now. Anyway, Emily didn't know just how the pencil would work. She wondered if Pete knew for sure.

At first the tunnel went through soft wet cement. Emily's feet sank into it with each step. The flashlight gave just enough light to keep her from bumping into the mushy walls. She thought of

Dick running through the tunnel in the dark. Emily tried to go faster.

In a little while the floor was dry, but it was very rough underfoot. The way was crooked now. Emily had to duck under slats of wood and squeeze between chunks of plaster.

The darkness was fading into a kind of twilight. Up ahead there was light.

Emily came to the end of the tunnel. She stepped out onto a hard floor. It was made of the biggest tiles Emily had ever seen.

In front of her there was a huge metal paw like the foot of a lion. It was holding up an enormous old-fashioned bathtub.

Emily had walked into the bathroom of the house next door.

A dim light came from a dirty skylight in the bathroom ceiling. Emily turned off her flashlight and put it back into her pocket.

She didn't like being in Mr. Dooley's house. It would be awful if he saw her there.

But where was Dick? Emily walked all around the huge room. She didn't see him anywhere.

The bathroom door was open. Emily went out into a hall. It was a lot like the hall in her own house. But the floor here wasn't shiny the way it was at home. Mr. Dooley didn't wash it very often, Emily thought.

A cockroach ran along the baseboard. Emily hated roaches. This one was bigger than her feet. She caught sight of a giant spider dangling by a thread from the ceiling.

Emily walked toward the stairs at the end of the hall. They were very big now that she was so small.

Someone was lying face-down on the top step. Emily's heart seemed to stop for an instant.

It was her brother!

She ran over and kneeled down beside him. "Dick, are you hurt?"

He turned his head to look at her. "Em!"

"Why are you lying down?" Emily asked.

"I'm trying to figure out the best way to get down these stairs," Dick told her.

"Why do you want to go downstairs?" Emily wanted to know.

"Domino ran down there," Dick said. "Mr. Dooley will do something terrible to him if he catches him. You know how he hates cats."

Emily saw that each of the stair steps was taller than she was. She pointed to the baseboard that slanted down the wall beside the stairs. "Why don't we slide down?"

"We'll have to hang our legs over the steps and go down sideways," Dick said.

Emily climbed onto the board. She grabbed Dick's hand to pull him up beside her.

They started sliding, using their hands as brakes. Halfway down they slipped off the board onto a little landing. Dick jumped to his feet and ran to climb onto the baseboard that went the rest of the way down the stairs. Emily came after him.

They began to slide faster. At the bottom of the stairs, Dick shot off the board onto the floor. Emily fell on top of him.

The two children stood up. They were in a dark hall. Dick rubbed his elbow. "Ouch! I landed on my funnybone."

"Sh-sh!" Emily pulled Dick back against the wall.

Someone was coming down the hall. But all Emily and Dick could see were two huge bedroom slippers walking toward them.

The slippers went right by and walked into the living room.

"That's Mr. Dooley," Dick said. "We'd better keep out of his sight."

The children tiptoed the other way down the hall.

They went past a gloomy dining room. There were six heavy chairs. A bowl of dusty wax fruit was set in the middle of the big table. The room looked as if nobody ever ate there.

At the end of the hall they came to a swinging door. Dick and Emily pushed as hard as they could. The door swung just wide enough to let them squeeze into the kitchen at the back of the house.

The kitchen smelled of stale coffee grounds and bacon grease.

Dick looked up at the grimy window. "Mr. Dooley can see into our yard from there. I'll bet he's always spying on us."

Emily had the creepy feeling that someone was watching them now. She grabbed Dick's arm. "Look!"

Two enormous eyes were shining in the dark shadows under the kitchen table.

It was a summer day. But Emily felt cold all over.

She was afraid to move. She just kept staring into the shadows. Little by little her eyes became used to the gloom. She could make out the shape of a huge cat crouched under the kitchen table.

It was Domino! His sharp teeth gleamed. And his claws looked like long knives. Emily was not much bigger than a mouse now. And she knew exactly how a mouse must feel.

Domino crawled out from under the table. His pink nose twitched. Emily held her breath.

Dick reached up and tickled the cat's

chin. "Smell my hand, Domino. Don't you know me?"

The cat pricked up his ears. He began to purr. The noise sounded so loud that Emily expected Mr. Dooley to come rushing into his kitchen to see what was going on there.

"Sh-sh, Domino." Emily was ashamed to have been afraid of the big cat. She gently stroked his soft chest.

The cat arched his back and stretched. He looked around the kitchen.

There was a bowl of leftover stew on the table. Domino jumped up and walked over to the bowl.

He took one sniff and drew back. Then he shook his paw and leaped to the floor. The next minute the cat marched to the swinging door, butted it open with his head, and slipped out of the kitchen.

"Hurry, Em! We've got to keep Domino away from the living room. Mr. Dooley's in there." Dick ran to the door. Together Dick and Emily pushed their way into the hall.

Domino had already reached the dining room door. He stopped to look inside. Emily and Dick raced down the hall toward him.

The children's feet pattered on the bare floor. The cat turned his head to see where the sound was coming from. He crouched, ready to spring. His sharp claws were curved and ready.

"It's us, Domino!" Emily yelled.

The cat yawned. He pulled his claws back inside his soft paws.

"If you yell like that, Em," Dick whispered, "Mr. Dooley will hear you."

"Domino," Emily said, "how about giving us a ride?"

"That's a great idea, Em." Dick

walked over to the black and white cat and rubbed his furry side.

Domino lay flat on the floor. Dick climbed onto his back. "Come on, Em."

Emily ran over and scrambled up behind her brother. She lay on her stomach and held tight to the cat's fur.

Dick sat astride Domino's neck, as if he were riding a horse. "We're better off here where he won't think we're something to eat. Giddyap, Domino!"

The cat leaped to his feet and went tearing down the hall. Dick bounced up and down. Emily was afraid that at any minute she'd slide off onto the floor.

"Whoah!" Dick tried to stop the cat. But he was too late.

Domino galloped into the living room.

Emily lay flat on the cat's back. She tried to hide in his black and white fur. Dick leaned against Domino's neck and pretended to be part of the cat.

Domino ran into Mr. Dooley's living room and sat down on the rug.

Dick and Emily expected Mr. Dooley to let out a yell and come rushing over to them.

There was no sound except the loud ticking of the tall clock in the corner of the room.

Emily looked around. The sunlight filtered through dirty windows onto the rug. All the furniture was old and worn. A newspaper was spread open on the sofa where someone had been reading it. And there was a cup and saucer on the coffee table. But no one was in the room now.

"Hey, Em, look at that!" Dick pointed to a table placed where the sunlight was not too strong.

Emily saw a big shiny glass tank on the table. The tank was full of water, and all sorts of plants were growing there. Little bright-colored fish were swimming in and out among the green stems.

Domino got up from the rug. He marched over to the table.

The cat looked up to see how far he had to jump. Then he gave one spring and landed right beside the glass tank. Domino stood on his hind legs and put his front paws on the rim.

"Now we know why Mr. Dooley doesn't like cats," Dick said.

"Leave the fish alone, Domino," Emily begged.

The cat didn't seem to hear her. He rested his chin on the edge of the tank and looked down into the water.

"Come on, Domino," Dick said. "Let's get out of here before Mr. Dooley comes back."

Domino didn't move. He seemed to have forgotten everything but the fish.

"I don't think he remembers that we're here," Emily said.

"I'll remind him." Dick climbed up the cat's neck onto his head. He grabbed hold of the edge of the cat's ear and leaned over to shout into it.

Domino felt something on his ear. He turned his head to one side and gave it a shake.

Dick started sliding. He made a grab for one of the cat's whiskers. But it slipped through his fingers. Splash!

Dick fell head over heels into the fish tank. Emily saw him struggling among the floating green plants on the surface of the water. A moment later he sank under them and disappeared.

Emily could swim better than Dick. She had to save him. And there was no time to lose. She grabbed hold of the cat's fur and pulled herself up onto his head.

Domino was still staring at the place in the water where Dick had fallen in. He didn't seem sure just what had happened.

Emily stood on her toes on the cat's head. She leaned over and dived into the tank.

Emily tried to dive between the plants in the fish tank. But she wasn't a very good diver, and she belly-flopped right into the middle of a tangle of floating grass. One long strand twined around the leg of her jeans. Emily tried to tear it off, but it was tough and wiry. She had to stop and tread water while she unwound the slippery grass. It seemed an age before she was free. She had to find Dick!

Emily took a deep breath and swam down into the tank. But she kept bobbing to the top of the water. She grabbed a plant stem and pulled herself down. It was like climbing a tree upside-down.

The tank seemed much bigger now

that Emily was in it. When she reached the bottom she still had to hold on to the plant to keep from bobbing up again.

Suddenly someone grabbed Emily's shoulders and hung on. She was so startled that she let go of the plant stem. At once she floated to the top of the water.

Emily turned her head to see who was clinging to her.

It was Dick. "You float like a cork, Em. I'm sure glad you came along. I couldn't have held my breath much longer."

"It's funny," Emily said. "You can't float, and I can't sink."

Dick grinned. "Together we ought to be able to work out something. I saw some things I'd like to get a better look at. Hold on to me, Em. Maybe I can pull you down."

Now it was Emily's turn to hang on to Dick's shoulders. He kicked his feet hard and swam to the bottom of the tank.

Two fat goldfish with flowing tails swam in front of the children. Dick pointed to a pile of dark red rocks, but Emily whirled him around and started floating up. Dick hung on to her, and she towed him to the top of the water. They poked their faces out and gulped for air.

"That was a *castle*, Em," Dick said. "I want to explore it."

"So do I," Emily told him. "But I had to get my breath back. I'm ready now."

"Come on, then." Dick slipped down through the water, pulling Emily along behind him.

When they came to the castle, Dick looked inside it. A school of tiny gup-

pies rushed out. They swarmed all over
Dick and Emily, nipping at their ears
and noses.

Dick started to slap at the little fish.

Emily grabbed his hands and pulled him to the top of the water.

Dick stuck his head out into the air. "Those things really bite!"

"Maybe they're hungry," Emily said.

"If it's feeding time," Dick told her, "Mr. Dooley will be coming to dump dried flies and ants' eggs in the tank."

Emily had forgotten all about Mr. Dooley. "We'd better get out of here." She looked up at the smooth straight sides of the tank. "But how are we going to do it?"

"I'm out already," she heard Dick say.

The next moment something hooked onto Emily's shirt. She tried to slip out of the shirt, but she was caught fast. Emily felt herself lifted high into the air.

Emily looked up into two huge un-blinking eyes. "Domino!"

The cat put her down on the table beside the fish tank. Emily tried to get up, but her shirt was still caught on one of Domino's claws. He held his paw very still while Emily unhooked her shirt from the sharp point. When she was free, Emily got to her feet.

Dick was lying on the table near her. He was still trying to get loose from Domino's other front paw. Emily went to help him.

When Dick was off the hook, he took a good look at the cat's claw. "Suppose he missed and stuck it into *me!* Let's go home and change back to our right size, Em."

"How are we going to get upstairs?" Emily asked. "We can't slide *up.*"

"Maybe Domino can give us some more help," Dick said. "He's done pretty well so far."

"We never even thanked him for getting us out of the fish tank." Emily reached up to stroke Domino under the chin. Then she climbed onto his back and sat down.

Dick took his place astride the cat's neck. "Take us back to our own house, Domino," he said.

Domino jumped softly off the table. He ran across the living room to the hall and started up the stairs.

Emily held tight to the cat's fur and bounced up and down. "Mr. Dooley must be upstairs," she said. "Watch out, Domino."

The cat went silently up the stairs and down the dusty hall to the big bathroom. He squeezed through the crack in the wall behind the old bathtub. There was hardly enough room for the cat. Emily and Dick crouched low on his back.

"I'd forgotten how dark and creepy it is in here," Dick said. "I hope one of those giant cockroaches doesn't fall on us."

Emily pulled her little red flashlight out of her pocket. She wasn't sure it would work after being in the fish tank. She turned it on. It lit up the dark tunnel. "Is this better?"

Dick grinned. "Much. *Seeing* a roach isn't nearly as scary as *feeling* it."

Domino picked his way through the crooked passage. He stepped around wooden slats and climbed over chunks of old plaster. When he came to the wet cement, the cat stopped and shook each paw in turn. Then he went on again.

Emily and Dick saw a glimmer of

light. A moment later Domino stepped out of the hole Pete had made. He lay down on the floor of the shower stall.

"We're home!" Emily climbed off the cat's back. She clicked off the flashlight and put it back into her pocket. "I'm soaking wet, but it doesn't seem to have hurt the flashlight."

"I'm wet too." Dick slid to the ground. "What a good cat you are, Domino! I know you hate water."

Domino turned his head and licked the damp place on his back. Then he leaped over the sill of the shower and trotted out of the pink bathroom.

"I hate to think of him having to stay outdoors in all kinds of weather and having to catch birds and squirrels for food," Emily said. "I wish we could find a good home for him."

The magic pencil was lying on the floor of the shower. Dick ran over to it. "It's as big as a log, Em. I can't even lift it."

Emily looked at the pencil. How could she have been so stupid? Even if she could have lifted the pencil, the blunt point was too thick to write on anything as small as Dick's arm, or her own.

"What'll we do now, Em?" Dick asked. "We can't reach the doorknob to let Pete into the house when he comes back. Dad's going to have a fit when he sees this shower. And I'll bet Mom won't like us being this size at all. We won't be able to load the dishwasher for her."

Emily didn't answer. She was climbing over the high sill of the shower door. Dick gave her a boost. Then she turned around and helped him over. They ran down the hall to the top of the stairs and slid down the slanting baseboard to the floor below.

The stepladder was standing where Emily had put it on the dropcloth in the living room when they came home from their picnic.

"You should have left it on its side," Dick told her. "This way we need a rope." He ran to the kitchen and looked up at the drawer in the cabinet. "Mom keeps string in there."

The drawer was open just wide enough for Dick to wiggle down into it — if only he could get up there.

Emily pried open the cupboard at

the bottom of the cabinet. "Give me a hand, Dick."

Together they pulled out a saucepan and turned it over. Dick climbed on the pan and from there stepped onto the handle of the cupboard. He swung himself to the top of the cupboard door. Now he could step onto the ledge of the cabinet.

Dick walked across the ledge and let himself down into the drawer. "It's dark in here. I wish I had your flashlight."

Emily heard him rustling around like a mouse. Then she saw his hand gripping the top edge of the drawer. A moment later, Dick came crawling out. He had a coil of string looped over his arm. "Here, catch!"

Dick threw the string to Emily. Then he dropped from the ledge to the top of the cupboard door and on down to the floor.

The string seemed like a heavy rope. Together they carried it to the living room. Emily got down on all fours at the foot of the ladder. "Stand on my back."

Dick pulled himself onto the lowest step. "Hand me the rope." He tied it around the step and Emily shinnied up to join him.

Step by step they climbed the ladder. When Dick reached the first red step, he said, "My head feels awful. It never felt this bad before." He tossed one end of the rope over the step. Emily had to tie it by herself. Dick closed his eyes and held tight to the step. "Hurry, Em!"

"It's because we're so small," Emily thought. "The magic is too strong for us. And Dick is smaller than I am."

Emily climbed the rope onto the red

step. "We want to go where Pete is," she said.

Dick's face was very white. He looked sick.

"Grab the rope," Emily said.

Dick leaned against her. "I can't, Em. My head hurts too much."

Emily's head felt worse than it ever had in all her life. She grabbed the rope with one hand and held on to Dick with the other. The ladder seemed much taller than a house. The rope cut into Emily's hand.

She dragged Dick off the red step and tried to hang on to the rope. But she lost her grip on it.

Emily held tight to her brother and closed her eyes. The two children tumbled off the ladder.

It seemed to Emily as if they had been falling for ages. She wondered if they'd ever hit the ground.

And then, thump! Emily and Dick landed on something warm and not nearly as hard as what Emily had been expecting.

She opened her eyes and saw what seemed to be an enormous, dirty thumb.

It took the two children a few moments before they realized what had happened.

They had been caught by two huge hands!

Dick looked up. "Pete!"

Emily peeked between the big fingers. The plumber was standing next to the ladder on the front stoop of Emily and Dick's house.

Pete stared down at them. "You must have been fooling with my pencil. I wondered what happened to it."

"You left it on the kitchen table," Emily said.

Pete grinned. "How were the graham crackers?"

"They were great. Thank you," Emily told him.

"Your pencil is in our bathroom now, Pete," Dick said. "We didn't hurt it."

"But you almost killed yourselves falling off my ladder," Pete said. "You ought to be more careful." He looked up and down the street. "Let's go inside before your neighbors see you like this. Do you have a key?"

Emily tugged at a string around her neck. She pulled the house key from under her shirt.

Pete looked at it. "That key's too small to open this door now. We're in trouble, kids."

"We could use the ladder," Emily said. "There's nobody around to see us."

"It's a handy ladder. But I never want people to see me fold it. Anyway I can't see how it would get the door open. Of course, if I had my pencil I

could just write *unlocked* on the door."
Pete grinned. "I've found there's a lot
you can do with that pencil if you put
your mind to it."

"Where'd you get the pencil?" Dick
asked.

"Same place I got the ladder," Pete
told him. "A friend gave them to me.
But she never said there was anything
special about them. I had to find that
out for myself."

"The way we did," Dick said.

Pete nodded.

"Did you ever stand on the red steps
of the ladder?" Emily asked him.

"Of course not! Red means *Danger!*"
The plumber frowned. "You must have
been standing on those steps when you
fell."

"If you stand on the red steps, Pete,"
Emily said, "you can go anywhere you
say you want to go."

"And we all want to go into the house," Dick said.

Pete put Emily into one of his pants pockets and Dick into the other. Then he climbed the ladder to the first red step. "My head feels funny," he said. "And my ears are buzzing."

Emily's head felt as if it would crack in half. She was sure Dick's felt worse. "We want to be back in our own house," she said.

"Nothing's happened." Pete backed off the red step.

Emily's head felt better at once.

Pete backed all the way down the ladder and stepped off at the bottom. He looked around.

They were on the dropcloth in the living room right under the hole in the ceiling.

Emily started to climb out of Pete's pocket.

"Take it easy, kids." Pete pulled the children out of his pockets. "We'd better do something about your size before you get into any more trouble." He carried Emily and Dick upstairs to the pink bathroom. "Where's the pencil?"

"In the shower," Dick said.

Pete held the children in one hand and picked up the pencil with the other. He looked hard at it. "Do you have a pencil sharpener?"

"There's one in the kitchen," Emily told him.

Pete took the children downstairs and put them on the kitchen table.

Dick looked at the box of graham crackers. "We took these along on our picnic. That's when we found out about the magic pencil."

"Picnic? Is that where you two were when I rang your doorbell?" Pete walked over to the pencil sharpener that was screwed to the cabinet.

"We borrowed your ladder," Emily told him. "I hope you don't mind."

Pete carefully sharpened the yellow pencil stub. "I spent the time looking for Mr. Checkers." The plumber came back to the table. "Now, where are the pencil marks on you?"

Dick and Emily showed him the numbers written on their arms.

"They're so small I can't read them." Pete gently rubbed the children's arms with the eraser on the end of the pencil. As soon as the rubber touched their skin, the numbers vanished.

"You first, Emily," Pete said. "Lie on your stomach and pull your shirt up off your back."

Emily did as she was told, and the plumber wrote on her bare back with the sharp point of his pencil. "It tickles," she said, trying not to giggle.

The next thing Emily knew her feet were sticking over the edge of the table. She wiggled off and dropped to the floor. "Pete!" she said. "How did you do it? I'm just as big as I was before. Exactly!"

The plumber smiled. "Watch!"

Now Dick lay on his stomach and Pete wrote with very small letters on his back:

RIGHT

SIZE

Emily looked at the kitchen clock. "It's almost five o' clock! Mother and Daddy will be home soon. Can you fix the wall of Daddy's shower, Pete?"

"I never got the bricks I need," Pete said. "The man didn't even have enough to finish the porch he was building. Nice guy. Turned out he knew my Uncle Harry."

Emily wasn't listening. She ran down the steps to the basement and came back with the paper bag of charcoal bricks. "I didn't believe you when you said you could use these."

Pete took the bag. "I'd forgotten all about them."

"Hurry, Pete," Emily said. "Dick and I will wait down here while you work."

Pete took the bag of charcoal and went upstairs.

Dick started after him. "I want to see what he does."

Emily grabbed his arm. "You stay here. Pete will start talking and never get the job done."

In almost no time they heard the plumber calling down the stairs. "Do you want to take a look?"

Dick and Emily raced upstairs to the pink bathroom. Pete handed Emily the bag of charcoal. She saw that he had written FULL on it.

They peeked into the stall shower. The ugly hole in the wall was gone. And all the shiny tiles were back in place.

Pete had gone downstairs. The children found him on his ladder in the living room. He was standing on the third step from the top.

The ceiling was white and smooth. There was no sign of the hole Pete had made in it. And the big damp place was gone.

Pete backed down the ladder and stepped off onto the dropcloth. Then he folded the ladder and put it into his shirt pocket. He looked at the big hammer lying on the dropcloth. "I'd better not forget this."

Pete took the yellow pencil stub from behind his ear and erased 28". Instead he wrote 1" on the hammer. He dropped it into his pocket with the ladder.

He wrote with his pencil on the corner of the dropcloth. At once it was no bigger than a handkerchief. Pete stuffed it into the back pocket of his pants. "I'll shake the plaster off it when I get outside," he said. "I have to go now."

"Thank you for helping us," Emily

said. "Are we going to see you again, Pete?"

The plumber smiled. "Of course. Tomorrow I'm doing a job for your neighbor." Pete walked into the front hall.

"Not mean old Mr. Dooley?" Dick said.

"He's not mean at all. I was talking to him while I was waiting for you to open your front door. He's just not used to kids." Pete laughed. "And he's scared to death of you two! I told him he'll like you when he gets to know you."

"What kind of job are you doing for Mr. Dooley?" Dick asked.

"He has trouble with his water pipes," Pete said. "The poor guy can't even wash his floors."

"Meow!" Domino came walking down the stairs.

"Mr. Checkers!" Pete cried. "Where

have you been? I've been looking all over for you."

"Is *he* Mr. Checkers?" Emily asked. "We call him Domino."

Pete leaned over to pet the cat. "Maybe he likes that name better. How about it, Domino? Shall we go home now?"

Domino purred and bumped his head against Pete's leg. Pete opened the front door and went out. The black and white cat followed him down the street.

Other books by Ruth Chew available in paperback
from Scholastic Book Services

Earthstar Magic (*Hardcover: Hastings House*)
The Hidden Cave
    (*Hardcover: Hastings House, as* The Magic Cave)
Magic in the Park
No Such Thing as a Witch
    (*Hardcover: Hastings House*)
Second-hand Magic (*Hardcover: Holiday House*)
The Secret Summer
    (*original title:* Baked Beans for Breakfast)
The Secret Tree House
Summer Magic
The Trouble with Magic (*Hardcover: Dodd Mead*)
The Wednesday Witch (*Hardcover: Holiday House*)
What the Witch Left (*Hardcover: Hastings House*)
The Wishing Tree (*Hardcover: Hastings House*)
Witch in the House (*Hardcover: Hastings House*)
Witch's Broom (*Hardcover: Dodd Mead*)
The Witch's Buttons (*Hardcover: Hastings House*)
The Witch's Garden (*Hardcover: Hastings House*)
The Would-be Witch (*Hardcover: Hastings House*)